THE GHOST NEXT DOOR

*How I Survived a Traumatic Depression
and Came Out the Other Side*

Cheryl Story

BALBOA.
PRESS

A DIVISION OF HAY HOUSE

Balboa Press books may be ordered through booksellers or by contacting:

Balboa Press
A Division of Hay House
1663 Liberty Drive
Bloomington, IN 47403
www.balboapress.com
1-(877) 407-4847

Because of the dynamic nature of the Internet, any web addresses or links contained in this book may have changed since publication and may no longer be valid. The views expressed in this work are solely those of the author and do not necessarily reflect the views of the publisher, and the publisher hereby disclaims any responsibility for them.

The author of this book does not dispense medical advice or prescribe the use of any technique as a form of treatment for physical, emotional, or medical problems without the advice of a physician, either directly or indirectly. The intent of the author is only to offer information of a general nature to help you in your quest for emotional and spiritual well-being. In the event you use any of the information in this book for yourself, which is your constitutional right, the author and the publisher assume no responsibility for your actions.

Any people depicted in stock imagery provided by Thinkstock are models, and such images are being used for illustrative purposes only. Certain stock imagery © Thinkstock.

Printed in the United States of America.

ISBN: 978-1-4525-7773-9 (sc)
ISBN: 978-1-4525-7774-6 (e)

Library of Congress Control Number: 2013912316

Balboa Press rev. date: 7/5/2013

On the day I called, You answered me; and made me bold with strength in my soul.

—Psalm: 138:3[1]

PREFACE

A ll of us have known people like this. They may be loved ones, friends, family members, or coworkers, but you have met them. Quite possibly it could be you yourself!

The "this" is depression or what experts call "clinical depression."

Daniel K. Hall-Flavin, MD, a psychiatrist at the Mayo Clinic, gives the following definition:"" Depression ranges in seriousness from mild, temporary episodes of sadness to severe, persistent depression. Doctors use the term "clinical depression" to describe the more severe form of depression, also known as "major depression" or "major depressive disorder." For a diagnosis of clinical depression, you must meet the symptom criteria spelled out in the *Diagnostic and Statistical Manual of Mental Disorders (DSM)*. The *DSM* is a guidebook used to diagnose mental illness in the United States.

Clinical depression symptoms may include

- depressed mood most of the day, nearly every day,
- loss of interest or pleasure in most activities,
- significant weight loss or gain,
- sleeping too much or not being able to sleep nearly every day,
- slowed thinking or movement that others can see,
- fatigue or low energy nearly every day,
- feelings of worthlessness or inappropriate guilt,
- loss of concentration or indecisiveness, and
- recurring thoughts of death or suicide.

To meet the criteria for clinical depression (called major depression in the *DSM)*, you must have five or more of the above symptoms over a two-week period. At least one of the symptoms must be either a depressed mood or a loss of interest or pleasure. Keep in mind, some types of depression may not fit this strict definition.

Clinical depression causes noticeable disruptions in daily life, such as work, school, or social activities. It can affect people of any age or sex, including children. It isn't the same as depression caused by a loss (such as the death of a loved one), substance abuse, or a medical condition such as a thyroid disorder. Clinical depression symptoms usually improve with psychological counseling, antidepressant medications, or a combination of the two. Even severe depression symptoms usually improve with treatment."[2] It is easy to ignore the symptoms, as they blend in silently, not wanting anyone to hear or see them. Many times you avert your eyes, as it causes you discomfort to even see the terror within caused by clinical depression.

You may avoid people with depression out of fear, or maybe you feel you lack the soothing words to help them out of their misery, if only for a short time. But avoid them you do. We do not mean to avoid them, yet we do because it is easier than facing them. Viewing sadness or raw depression causes us our own discomfort; it may show weakness in those suffering or open an old wound we ourselves have had.

I know this all too well, as I become one of the fallen myself!

ACKNOWLEDGMENTS

This is dedicated to some very special people who helped me out of the shadows and back to the living. Tim and George, there have never been two people who have done more, and my love for you is true! You both are most certainly angels. Thank you for bringing me back from the abyss!

To Cynthia, one of the most generous, loyal people I shall ever meet, I will never have words—or enough time—to thank you for all you do. I love you as well.

And then, again, to my mom, Norma Hershey Winchester, who is watching, I love you and miss you much. I will always be grateful to you for my love of the written word.

Finally, to Wendy Herrington, my first contact at Balboa, it was because of you that this book was finally written. You helped open my eyes to the reality of what this work may mean to many. I am deeply grateful!

INTRODUCTION

"During the midst of the darkest night, act
as though morning has already come."

—The Talmud

You will not find your typical ghost story here: no bumps or screams in the night. There is no eerie visage of some dark figure. Instead, this is a story about how I became a ghost due to depression and about what depression can do to a person's life.

The words and events within this book have been silent until now. All that is revealed is true and actual. It is long past time that the ghost I became and the dark shadow accompanying depression be brought to the light. Light not only aids in viewing but also brings hope.

After a sudden, alarming departure and the end of a sixteen-year relationship, my world was turned upside down.

This narrative reveals my journey to the darkest place and the ghost I became.

It is my most heartfelt desire that my journey somehow can bring light and hope to others who feel the ghost at their door.

Part One

BEFORE THE GHOST

The fall of 2006 started as one expects when living on the west coast of Florida. Days were still humid and hot; no leaves were changing. Life for me was continuing as always. I had recently started a new job and had to travel a hundred miles a day round-trip. But the job promised advancement, and the pay was decent (as decent as you might expect in sunny Florida).

I lived with my then-partner (of almost sixteen years) in a small but comfortable home in a relatively quiet, uneventful neighborhood. We had each other, our three schnauzers, and friends, and life was good. At the same time I was beginning my new job, I was also taking classes online to finish my long-overdue BA degree in English literature. I was, for all intents and purposes, happy, and my life was full.

In late October, my partner was going away on a short trip to Michigan to visit with an old friend and get some well-needed time away from the seemingly endless task of caring for an elderly, ill mother. My new job and course online prevented me from going, obviously. What seemed an innocent period apart would change, very shortly, life as I then knew it to be.

Now looking back to the time and the events that unraveled, I recall a particular night. While walking the dogs, I suddenly had a queer feeling. A shudder went through me, and I knew that somehow, some way, a change was coming. And come it did. Had I listened to that whispering, still voice within, could I have possibly changed what lay ahead? Even now I think not.

On my partner's return, I sensed some small changes but swept them away, telling myself I was seeing something that just wasn't there. But as the time slipped into November, my fears or delusions of a lurking, hidden problem began to surface ever so slowly into a reality I had not wanted to see. Even confronting and questioning my partner didn't bring me any real answers. Deep inside, I knew something was not right, and my world seemed to change before my very eyes.

As Thanksgiving drew closer and things seemed to continue with no real answers, I finally met the situation head-on. My partner then finally stated that while we would always be the truest of friends, we were basically through. I recall the cajoling, the tears, and my arguments that we would fix whatever it was that had been broken, but to no avail. I asked if there was someone else, but no, that was not the reason; it was just past time, and there was nothing either of us could do to repair time. I remember stating that we could get counseling, together or separately; again, that was too little, too late.

During this precarious time, I spoke of this to no one—not my mother, who was and always had been more a friend than a mom, nor to anyone else. I still did not know many of my colleagues at work well enough to confide in them, and for the most part they were used to seeing me as positive. This would change very soon. Four days after Thanksgiving (which we did not celebrate together as we had in normal, different times), my partner, and one of our dogs, got in the car and drove off. And that was it.

And me—I spent most of December still attempting to mend fences that no longer could be mended. My friends George and Tim were the only ones I told about my personal situation. During the Christmas holidays, I even lied to my mother and said that my partner and I would be out of town. I contacted a counselor, thinking this might get us back on our feet. It did not, but it was the sanest choice I ever made. I had no idea how important that call would be and what an important role it would play in my next journey.

And so I began my journey to depression and the painful havoc that became my new life.

THE GHOST NEXT DOOR

You would not see me—of that I made sure. Cloaked in darkness at all times, I would do the mundane, necessary items of the day: retrieve the mail, take out the trash, walk the dog. Always confident that no one would know I was there, I didn't even know for sure that I, myself, existed. Many times I could be found, sitting in the darkness inside my home, making no noise and showing no signs of life. I sat in my protective shell, cocoon-like, waiting, usually crying. Sobs writhed through me.

I know my neighbors must have wondered, even shuddered, at what was happening within my house, what evil might prevail. My home was always in darkness; if they looked closely, they might have seen a low candle glowing or perhaps heard whimpering or my screaming.

I was the ghost next door!

When I was forced to leave my home (only out of sheer necessity), I drove through the dark streets, mindless of the traffic or other people around me. Through the days and hours, and eventually months, that I held the demons within, somehow (and yes, miraculously) I was able to keep my job, collecting on delinquent mortgages. When I did encounter people throughout the day at work, I somehow always managed to slip quickly away, avoiding contact of any kind. Conversation with others of any type, even the simplest of greetings, could—and at times did—spiral me into panic, or worse, tears.

At the end of the day, I was desperate to get back to my shell, my safe haven. Only then could I allow the sobs, the silent screaming, to begin anew.

I was the ghost next door!

This haunted house, trapped in unfathomable, painful darkness, was not chosen by me. But no one would choose this gut-wrenching, stark sadness. There were hundreds of times I would wake from stolen moments of much-needed sleep and wonder at the depths of my sadness. I questioned the whats and the whys. How did I allow myself to become this way? How did I give another person the power to rip my life apart at the seams? And how was it that my breath still came, without reminding myself to do that very thing? I learned that just breathing can be the hardest thing of all. I yelled at God sometimes, waiting for answers. I heard none. Yet somehow I knew the answer seemed to be that I had simply allowed this.

I was the ghost next door!

When I first felt this depression envelop me, when the darkness began its vast descent, I was surprised. I was surprised not only by the depths of this depression but also by the fact that I had been visited by depression at all. There had been other hard times in my life: difficult days, heartrending events, losses, and deaths of loved ones. But I had always prevailed before. In fact, many people considered me a rock, a source of strength in times of woe. This time, however, through a sequence of events and circumstances not chosen by me, I found my way to depression.

I was the ghost next door!

In my new home, my haunted house, there was no laughter and no joy. There was no light at all. Hope, which is our very thread to life and to light itself, had seemingly slipped through my fingertips and escaped me. A shell of my former self, I gave way and grew ever closer to the darkness I now welcomed as friend.

I was the ghost next door.

I wore these new, translucent robes well. Their shackles enveloped me and stretched through to every fiber of my being. The stark, deep, entrenching darkness encroached its way into every aspect of myself. And now more often than not, it seemed much easier just to end my life, which held so very little meaning for me. The thought of ending my life came easily and often. When one feels that one's life has been ripped away and one's very heart is gone, death seems an obvious end.

I was, after all, the ghost next door.

There were many times, late in the night, alone in my

own stillness, that the thought of suicide beckoned to me. Somehow it seemed fitting to me. It alone would quiet the despair and the utter futility I now viewed as my life. I even remember thinking once that I could just go outside behind my house and lie there quietly, waiting to be gone forever, to be done with all this sorrow and pain. Today, I do not recall what prevented me from taking my own life. I do know it was providence, and perhaps a visit from an angel. For whatever purpose, whatever His reasoning, God did step in.

THE GHOST LINGERS . . .

My life (if one could call it that) remained cast in shadows, and the tears continued to flow. I found solace only when I was safe within the quiet of my home. It was there and only there that I could give in to the darkness, wrapped up and hidden from the world. Here, in this quiet, I could give way to tortured sobs.

It should come as no surprise that in my haven, the darkness, I would rant, beg, and even plead with God. Often, I do not know exactly what I sought from Him, but ask I did. More often than I would like to admit, I would argue and, yes, even scream at God. But between the yelling and the sobs and the rants, I also began to pray. And still the ghost remained.

Depression is a mighty beast. It can knock us down to the ground and keep beating even after we are down for the count. It slithers and seeps into every single pore of our beings and gives no rest. Life ceases, halted for a time by this silent, cunning demon. It can and does affect every portion of our lives and touches the lives of those around us as well.

I spent many weeks and countless hours praying, scolding God, and even bargaining. Bargaining with what, you might ask. I did not know that either. What could I or anyone have to offer to God? Those answers would come to me much later.

These actions did not bring peace (yet), nor did they bring hope. Yet solace I sought, and solace I began to find. But still it seemed that I had become so insubstantial that I would never be solid again.

And still the ghost remained. But the ghost began to see a glimmer of …

There were times I was amazed at the tears. How much could one person cry? The abyss continued to wrap me in its fog. As the tears and darkness continued, so did my search for grace, God, and some kind of peace.

Somewhere from within, through the mists of tears and the darkness, I began to sense a change. As my ranting and praying continued, I began to feel a lifting and some ease in the pain. This ghost had enveloped and cloaked me for many months now, and at times it seemed destined to stay. When one becomes accustomed to darkness, one almost welcomes it. It seems to wrap you in some nether world of safety. Yet one realizes this is untrue. And somehow, at some point, something within me let go of this stranglehold. I began my ascent.

It was not immediate. It did not take minutes or hours— or even days! But climb I did, slowly, gasping for breath, and seeking the light. In reaching for that light, I began again to see a glimpse, a brief hint, of hope. I had begun to feel and to view within myself a quiet change. Slowly, I began to feel some of the depression lift from me.

After a time, I sensed that the ghost had begun to hope again. Somewhere within me I felt that somehow I had made it past the midnight hour, like the hands on the clock. This slow progression past midnight seemed to bring signals within me of quiet changes. I began to feel an awareness, a change in my inner spirit. We all, at one time or another, pass through a dark night. A new dawn brings with it a new vision. We begin to see new answers, possibilities not visualized in the darkest hours of night.

Loss is normal, even expected, in each of our lives. Being lost, however, is an entirely different journey. Feeling lost inspires intense fear. It is as if you are a young child in a mall, disconnected from your family. Being lost means not having hope; it means aimless wandering. And your cries for help in your anguish seemingly go unanswered. There is loss, and then there is being lost. My travel to the darkness included both.

THE GHOST
BECOMES WEARY . . .

I had somehow, after days and weeks, begun to feel a strengthening within me. I had a clearer view of the person I truly was and of the life I wanted to continue.

As light began to seep into and through the mists of the darkness, I was aware of myself beginning to emerge. The new self was small, stretching baby steps toward the light, crawling slowly to the end of this tunnel and away from the ghost. It is much like swimming in the dark waters of a lake. You are unable to see anything in front of you or around you at all. But instinctively you know that you must push upward toward the surface. There, gasping for breath, you are again free and surrounded by light.

The ghost does not want the light; it even shuns the light. It is quite happy with how things are and wants you to stay, forever, in the darkness. But like a swimmer in that dark lake, I had begun my ascent toward light, hope, and life. The ghost I had become, the ghost that had surrounded and shrouded me in darkness, grew ever wearier and then was gone.

Part Two

HOW I BECAME FREE FROM THE GHOST AND DARKNESS

This travel to the darkness is not mine alone. Many before and after me have taken this same road, though certainly not by choice. I am no expert in this journey. Any of us at any time could become a ghost too. The ghost that I had become may very well be familiar to you, now or at some point in your life.

It was several years later that I understood that the ghost had been silent within me for a very long time. Today I can honestly say that I count it as a blessing that my ghost appeared at all. If depression had not taken such complete control over me, I would likely not be here to write this at all. My time with the ghost taught me to seek help, to turn to others, and to know truly and very deeply that without God, I am utterly alone. It is not an easy thing to confess, but quite frankly, I most likely would have taken my own life long before now if not for the ghost.

The event that had catapulted me into impending darkness, as I stated earlier, caught me unaware. Someone who is unprepared for a storm can do little against the arrival of peril. Yet when I first felt the tentative approaching of the darkness, I began taking small steps to protect me from the coming storm.

How blessed we all are to have an inner knowledge, an intuition, that "still, small voice within," to aid us even in the darkest moments of our lives. Even as the ghost was lurking, that voice within me started to instruct and, yes, to protect. I had long held a firm, quiet faith in God. I knew without doubt that He existed and was here for us all. I was not a churchgoer and rather abhorred religion itself, instead believing that my church was the world around me and within. At the time of my descent into the abyss of deep depression, my relationship with God was shallow, at best.

As I began to feel more and more like a ghost, somehow I knew there were certain measures I had to take—and quickly. It was with apprehension that I pulled out a phone book and went to the directory for counselors. Because of the state of my relationship with religion itself, I did not want to seek help from a minister.

I was lucky (blessed) to find a counselor who was recommended by a Methodist church I contacted. As if planned, I found that her office was not far from my home.

I went to see her and continued meeting with her weekly, if not more often, for close to nine months. These sessions with her at first were traumatic in themselves and quite difficult. I am not one to speak of personal matters and prefer keeping them to myself or sharing them only with a trusted friend. There had always been things I did not share with my close family. And if I ever thought for a moment that something might worry my mother, I kept my thoughts to myself. So, these weekly meetings with the counselor were a huge first step, but they were also very, very necessary.

These sessions with Dr. Elizabeth became a vital portion of my week. At first much of them were spent crying. But as our talks took shape, I began to see not only who I was but also how misshapen my sixteen-year relationship had been. She helped me see my true self better than ever before and define mistakes made by me and others in my relationships. There is much to be said for speaking with someone who has no knowledge of any of the players in one's life and can offer true and insightful guidance. I will always be thankful to her and to the path that led me to her.

The next step was the most important of all. I had to begin the healing, to beat the ghost, to shed light where there had been none. As I have stated from the beginning, I continued to pray. When I was in my haven of darkness, I talked almost ceaselessly, often yelling as well. I asked God for His help. I implored Him to put His hand on my wrecked life, asking for the heartbreak to end and the pain to stop. At times I begged to be rid of the ghost that had become me. So much time was spent on my knees or literally throwing myself to the floor—crying, yes, but always praying. The words themselves, what I asked for specifically at any time, I do not recall—and yet it did not matter. I was praying! I didn't recognize at first how vital this act alone was, but it soon became my refuge, almost my life's blood.

And ever so slowly, quietly, without noticing at first, I began to see light and to feel it within me as well. A healing had begun; my soul and spirit were renewing themselves. Darkness began to slip away, and the hole within me started to fill. This slow ascent began to stir within me, and I started to feel that one so vital thing I thought I had lost forever: hope. Hope is a wondrous gift in our lives. When you have none, the emptiness of its loss leaves you in a huge, barren, thankless world. The ghost had vanished.

LIFE BEYOND THE GHOST

While it may seem hard for anyone to fathom, the exit of the ghost was at first a difficult transition. It was much like having to wear glasses and then starting to wear contacts. Somehow you keep looking for the glasses, even though you can now see fine without them. Or after having a cast removed from an arm or a leg, you still feel that it is there. Slowly, ever so gently, I brought myself back to the reality of life and all it entails. I still had difficulty being around crowds or a lot of noise, but slowly, quietly, I began my climb out of the abyss.

This experience taught me many things and brought about many realizations. I learned a great deal about myself and continue to do so. Writing this piece has itself awakened new memories, and I see huge changes within myself and in my daily interaction with others. Now, six years later, I know without doubt that the ghost will not visit me again.

I also know that it is through the grace of God that I am here to share this story. But the most important thing I learned from this trial and darkness is that we are never, ever alone. We all share in grace and in the highest love there is.

It is my extreme hope that my words will help you too to see the other side of midnight.

Part Three

THE GHOST AT YOUR DOOR

M uch of my strength before the ghost was allowed in was just a mask I had designed myself. We all sometimes feel we must put on a "happy face," even when it's not a true indicator of how we feel. We often feel we must hide our true feelings or thoughts in fear of revealing too much to the outside world. Each of us becomes adept at hiding from our loved ones, and most importantly from ourselves, the reality of our true selves. We feel fear, even shame, if we allow the outside world or those close to us to see the darkness within, to see and view despair of any kind.

The world we live in today does not treat kindly those who appear weak in any sense, let alone in their inner selves. On the national and local news, we see the horror children suffer at the hands of bullies. Young children and teens are picked on for appearing weaker to the other kids. Depression and mental illness should and must be addressed at a national level. We seemingly have progressed so far, yet so many issues that need to be brought to the forefront remain locked within the very ones who need help. We see much too often, in the United States especially, that mental illness and depression are not dealt with properly. Much too late, we learn the consequences of not paying attention to this, sadly, growing trend.

While depression and the deep darkness are difficult to speak of; speak you must. And speak loudly; do not stop until your voice is heard. One of the most glaring truths I learned while in that deep tunnel was that people, even friends and family members, tend to shy away and even run from the face of depression.

I implore you: If you recognize at any moment even a hint of the darkness or the approach of that ghost, talk to someone. I urge you to seek help, and above all start praying—as if your life depended upon it. Trust me, it does. It is vitally important to get a grip on this situation before it becomes, sadly, too late. And if the person who is going through this despair is a family member, sister, parent, coworker, or friend, offer help. Talk to your loved ones, get them to hear you, and let them know above all that someone cares.

Our lives here are too short to be swallowed up in this abyss. Each one of us on this grand planet is a gift, and we each have a gift to be shared with all. It is your God-given right and His ultimate wish that each of us have and share joy and a wonderful life!

IMPORTANT STATISTICS FOR THE UNITED STATES

At the time of this writing, "Suicide rates are up alarmingly among middle-aged Americans, according to the latest federal government statistics.

They show a 28 percent rise in suicide rates for people aged 35 to 64 between 1999 and 2010. Rates for children and younger adults, and people over 65, didn't change much over the same time, the Centers for Disease Control and Prevention reports.

"Most suicide research and prevention efforts have focused historically on youth and the elderly. This report's findings suggest that efforts should also address the needs of middle-aged persons," CDC researchers wrote in the agency's weekly report in death and disease."[3]

These numbers alone are glaring indicators of our turbulent times and lives.

My own story only skims the surface as to how deeply depression touches all of us. I know you have seen television commercials about antidepressants. Currently there are thirty-two known prescriptions to treat this illness. Yet these drugs do not always help. Too often, people who suffer from depression turn to suicide.

On September 24, 2012, the *Huffington Post* listed suicide as the leading cause of death by injury. The article goes on further: "The switch is a culmination of a decade- long trend; the rate of death by suicide increased by 15 percent over the past ten years, while the unintentional death by motor vehicle crash death rate dropped by 25 percent during the same period. Perhaps even more disturbing of all is that suicide is the fourth leading cause of death for children aged ten to fourteen and the third leading cause of death for young people aged fifteen to twenty-four."[4]

Of course, there is a difference between depression and sadness. We all will, and do from time to time, feel sad for many reasons. We suffer a loss of a loved one, a friend or relative moves far away, or a beloved pet dies. This sadness or grief is normal and sometimes can go on for several months. These are normal instances in our daily lives. We can feel sadness watching the six-o'clock news, but there are startling differences between sadness and depression.

These facts and sheer numbers astound me. They seem an epitaph, a marker on our current society and global community. If we cannot protect our own, our brightest, our children, what else is any of us to do, and what statements does this fact make about us? We have too many living in quiet, scalding desperation, and seemingly the ghost is winning.

But I declare and invoke, as one of its members, that these numbers must be attended to and squashed. As individuals and members of this great nation and world, we can and must act. Those actions must be bold and must start now. Our children, our relatives, and our friends deserve our action and deserve to be heard.

As stated in *A Course in Miracles*, "Nothing real can be threatened; nothing unreal exists; herein lies the peace of God." So be it!

SINCE THE GHOST HAS DEPARTED

It has been six years since I shook off the shackles of the ghost. I must report that I will never be sorry for this trial, nor will I regret the ghost. Much has changed since then—all for the better, I might add. Even today I still learn from the experience and recognize lessons, even epiphanies, I learned in my darkest hours.

One of the most startling points I learned was that, while it was my darkest time, it was not my first visit to the unknown depths. It took me several years to realize that there had been a very thin line between the darkness and the light for a very long time. This is the reason I implore all who recognize even a hint of their own experience in anything I have written to get help. Please ask, please seek, and please knock. Talk to someone, find healing, and look for the light that is there for us all—and *hope*!

There's a quote from the Talmud that simply states, "Every blade of grass has its angel that bends over it and whispers, Grow, grow." How much more will your angel do for you?

Perhaps the most vital truth I learned is that though we

are not alone, we do not need others to complete us. Yes, we all want and should have friends, partners, and spouses, but we do not need them to complete us, and they must not be our sole reason for life or our sole source of happiness. My joy, my happiness, my bliss, my truths, and my untruths should never be validated by anyone else but me. It is my sole responsibility, even my right, to obey that still, small voice within and complete myself.

Whatever your faith or lack thereof, this is a universal truth. When you can begin to accept this one great, epic truth, it truly will set you free. And this realization will lead you to your joy, give you great peace, and guide you well on your journey.

AFTERWORD

"If light is in your heart, you will find your way home."

—Rumi

I want to be clear to everyone that I hold no medical degrees, no psychiatry nor counseling degrees, and no certifications. I do not pretend to be an expert in any of the fields relating to depression, trauma, or mental illness.

This story I have shared about my life and events that occurred is true. I speak to you only as an everyday person, like any of you who may read this. I share this very personal admission in the hope that someone may find comfort and help from this book.

CITATIONS

1. New American Standard Bible (NASB),Copyright © 1960, 1962, 1963, 1968, 1971, 1972, 1973, 1975, 1977, 1995 by The Lockman Foundation. Psalm 138:3 in all English translations.
2. Hall-Flavin, Daniel, M.D. , assessed, April 21.2011, http://www.mayoclinic.com/health/clinical-depression/AN01057
3. Fox Maggie, Senior Writer, NBC News, assessed May 2, 2013 http://www.nbcnews.com/health/suicide-rates-go-middle-aged-cdc-finds-6C9742532?franchiseSlug=healthmain#suicide-rates-go-middle-aged-cdc-finds-6C9742532
4. http://www.huffingtonpost.com/2012/09/24/suicide-leading-cause-death-us_n_1909772.html

www.ingramcontent.com/pod-product-compliance
Lightning Source LLC
Chambersburg PA
CBHW050348290526
45785CB00006B/2688